MW00908826

YOU MU 1959 THIS

MILESTONES, MEMORIES,
TRIVIA AND FACTS, NEWS EVENTS,
PROMINENT PERSONALITIES &
SPORTS HIGHLIGHTS OF THE YEAR

TO : _____

FROM : _____

MESSAGE : _____

_____

selected and researched
by
mary a. pradt

WARNER ⬤ TREASURES ™

PUBLISHED BY WARNER BOOKS

A TIME WARNER COMPANY

Warner Books, Inc.
1271 Avenue of the Americas
New York, New York 10020

Warner Treasures is a
trademark of Warner Books, Inc.

A Time Warner Company

DESIGN:
CAROL BOKUNIEWICZ DESIGN
PRINTED IN SINGAPORE
FIRST PRINTING : MAY 1995
10 9 8 7 6 5 4 3 2 1
ISBN : 0-446-91035-X

America's first team of astronauts, seven men who were selected for the Project Mercury man-in-space program, were named by NASA in April. They were Scott Carpenter, Gordon Cooper, John Glenn, Gus Grissom, Walter Schirra, Alan Shepard, and Deke Slayton.

Alaska became the 49th state;

the first new state in 47 years, in January. The largest state, it is more than twice the size of Texas. The 49-star flag was to have a short run.

Hawaii, the youngest state, achieved statehood August 21, 1959.

President Eisenhower unfurled the 50-star flag at the White House; it would become the official flag July 4, 1960. The white 5-pointed stars are arranged in staggered rows—five 6-star rows and four 5-star rows.

HAWAII

THE SOVIET THREAT AND THE SPACE RACE DOMINATED THE NEWS.

newsreel

EISENHOWER USED HIS PRESTIGE TO TRY TO END THE EAST-WEST STALEMATE, MAKING GREAT EFFORTS AT DETENTE BY GOODWILL EXCHANGES WITH THE SOVIETS. NOTABLY, IN SEPTEMBER, SOVIET PREMIER KHRUSHCHEV MADE A 10-DAY TOUR OF THE U.S., FROM NEW YORK TO LOS ANGELES AND FROM SAN FRANCISCO TO DES MOINES. KHRUSHCHEV'S HOST IN IOWA WAS FARMER ROSWELL GARST, WHO WAS SO BESIEGED BY NEWSMEN THAT HE THREW SILAGE AT THEM.

Civil rights continued to be a major issue. Federal courts continued to strike down racial discrimination in public places. Protesting federal encroachment on their "states' rights," some Southerners put their stamps upside down on everything they posted, with the slogan "Invert Abe until states have rights."

3

In France in January, **Charles de Gaulle** became president of the Fifth Republic. He was swept into office by more than 75 percent of the vote and was elected primarily because of the crisis in Algeria. De Gaulle started pushing for greater French control in NATO and for the Allies to support his Algerian policy.

The Soviets outpaced America in the space race. They managed to send the Lunik II rocket around the moon and to photograph its never-before-seen far side.

headlines

international

IN JANUARY, FIDEL CASTRO'S FORCES TOOK COMPLETE CONTROL IN CUBA.

The International Olympic Committee voted in May to withdraw recognition from Nationalist China as no longer being representative of the whole country. Communist China would be allowed to compete in the games scheduled for 1960 in Squaw Valley. The U.S. was incensed by this decision, and the House voted to withdraw $400,000 support from those Olympics.

The day the music died—on February 3, successful young rock artists **Buddy Holly**, 22; **J. P. "the Big Bopper" Richardson**, 24; and **Richie Valens**, 17, were killed in a plane crash near Mason City, Iowa. The teen idols' biggest hits, all recent million-sellers, were, respectively, "Peggy Sue" and "That'll Be the Day," "Chantilly Lace," and "Donna" and "La Bamba."

cultural
milestones

THE FAD OF STUFFING PHONE BOOTHS, WHICH FIRST STARTED IN SOUTH AFRICA, WAS THE RAGE ON AMERICAN COLLEGE CAMPUSES IN THE SPRING OF 1959.

Congressional hearings revealed that most of the TV quiz shows had been "**fixed**" for years. Contestants on "Tic Tac Dough" and "The $64,000 Question" had been fed answers; "Name That Tune" winners had heard the songs hummed before the show. Even Charles Van Doren, a Columbia University professor who had won $129,000 on "21," was tainted by the quiz-show scandals. The government began to look into regulating TV more tightly.

"Bonanza," the first Western to be broadcast in color, premiered on NBC in September. CBS debuted **"The Many Loves of Dobie Gillis,"** as well as **"The Twilight Zone." "The Untouchables"** premiered on ABC.

THERE WERE 44,462,000 AMERICAN HOMES WITH TV, OR 86.3%. OF TV HOMES, 4,400,000 HAD MORE THAN ONE TV SET.

1. "Gunsmoke" (CBS)
2. "Wagon Train" (NBC)
3. "Have Gun Will Travel" (CBS)
4. "The Danny Thomas Show" (CBS)
5. "The Red Skelton Show" (CBS)
6. "Father Knows Best" (CBS)
7. "77 Sunset Strip" (ABC)
8. "The Price Is Right" (NBC)
9. "Wanted: Dead or Alive" (CBS)
10. "Perry Mason" (CBS)
11. "The Real McCoys" (ABC)
12. "The Ed Sullivan Show" (CBS)
13. "The Bing Crosby Show" (ABC)
14. "The Rifleman" (ABC)
15. "The Ford Show" (NBC)
16. "The Lawman" (ABC)
17. "Dennis the Menace" (CBS)
18. "Cheyenne" (ABC)
19. "Rawhide" (CBS)
20. "Maverick" (ABC)

"Rocky and His Friends"

debuted on ABC September 29, 1959. Bullwinkle the Moose and Rocky the flying squirrel costarred. Their teamwork helped them triumph over adversaries Mr. Big, the evil midget; Boris Badenov ("long for bad"), Russian agent; and his aide, Natasha Fataly ("long for fatal"). Popular cartoon segments included Fractured Fairy Tales and the saga of Canadian Mountie Dudley Do-Right and his arch-enemy, Snidely Whiplash.

milestones

Many Americans sat by their TV sets, fascinated, watching the wedding ceremonies of **Crown Prince Akihito of Japan** and a commoner, **Miss Michiko Shoda** in April. It was the first marriage of a prince and a commoner in the 619-year history of the throne. Another fairy-tale romance that intrigued people worldwide was the courtship between Stephen C. Rockefeller, son of the New York governor and heir to Rockefeller bucks, and Anne Marie Rasmussen, a young Norwegian woman who had worked as a maid for the Rockefellers. They were married in Norway on August 22. NBC newsman Chet Huntley married Miss Lewis Tipton Stringer, a former weather commentator, March 7. Raul Castro, 28, married fellow revolutionary Vilma Espin, 24, whose nom de guerre was Deborah, January 20 in Santiago de Cuba.

D E A T H S

Former Secretary of State **John Foster Dulles**, Ike's chief Cold War strategist, died in May after a two-year battle with cancer. Avidly anti-Communist, Dulles defined the policy of brinkmanship and was widely admired. He was awarded the Medal of Freedom a month before. **Cecil B. DeMille**, the creator of movie spectaculars, died January 21 of a heart ailment in Hollywood. **Lou Costello**, comedic partner of Bud Abbott, died in March. **Duncan Hines**, American gourmet, died March 15 at 78. **Lester Young**, jazz great, and hard-boiled novelist **Raymond Chandler** also died in March. **Frank Lloyd Wright**, the century's most important architect, died April 9 at 89. Renowned stage actress **Ethel Barrymore** died in June at 79. Screen idol **Errol Flynn** died October 14. Blues legend **Billie Holiday** died at 44, after years of drug abuse and dissipation. **George Reeves**, who had portrayed Superman in more than 100 TV episodes, shot and killed himself at 45 on June 16 in Hollywood, three days before he was to marry a New York socialite. Pulitzer Prize-winning playwright **Maxwell Anderson** died at 70 on February 28, of a stroke.

celeb births

SARAH, DUCHESS OF YORK, the former Sarah Ferguson, was born October 15.

RIGOBERTA MENCHÚ, Guatemalan human rights activist and Nobel Peace Prize winner, was born in 1959.

IRENE CARA, singer, was born March 18.

SHEENA EASTON, performer, was born April 27.

RANDY TRAVIS, country great, was born May 4.

SHAUN CASSIDY, actor and singer, was born September 27.

EARVIN "MAGIC" JOHNSON, basketball legend, was born August 13.

JOHN MCENROE, tennis star, was born February 16.

JIM MCMAHON, football player, was born August 21.

LAWRENCE TAYLOR, football player, was born February 4.

RONNIE LOTT, football player, was born May 8.

FRED COUPLES, top golfer, was born October 3.

RYNE SANDBERG, baseball player, was born September 18.

SUSAN FALUDI, controversial journalist, was born April 18.

KYLE MACLACHLAN, actor, who rose to fame with David Lynch's *Dune* and *Blue Velvet*, as well as "Twin Peaks," was born February 22.

LINDA BLAIR, actress, whose first big break came with *The Exorcist*, was born January 22.

ROSANNA ARQUETTE, actress, was born August 10.

MACKENZIE PHILLIPS, actress and singer, was born November 10.

BRONSON PINCHOT, actor and comedian, was born May 20.

TRACEY ULLMANN, comic actress, was born December 30.

JESSICA HAHN, infamous secretary, was born July 7.

MARIE OSMOND, singer, was born in Utah on October 13.

FLORENCE GRIFFITH JOYNER, track legend, was born December 21.

TIM BURTON, director, was born in Burbank, sometime in 1959.

50 hit music

1. **mack the knife** Bobby Darin
2. **the battle of new orleans** Johnny Horton
3. **venus** Frankie Avalon
4. **stagger lee** Lloyd Price
5. **the three bells** Browns
6. **lonely boy** Paul Anka
7. **come softly to me** Fleetwoods
8. **smoke gets in your eyes** The Platters
9. **heartaches by the number** Guy Mitchell
10. **sleep walk** Santo & Johnny

11. **kansas city** Wilbert Harrison
12. **a big hunk o' love** Elvis Presley
13. **mr. blue** Fleetwoods
14. **why** Frankie Avalon
15. **the happy organ** Dave "Baby" Cortez.

Danceability was key. Some of these slower tunes lent themselves to line dances like the Continental and the Stroll.

Other Top 10 tunes included: Paul Anka's "Put Your Head on My Shoulder," the Crests' "16 Candles," Connie Francis's "Lipstick on Your Collar," Ricky Nelson's "Never Be Anyone Else But You," Sarah Vaughan's "Broken-Hearted Melody," Fabian's "Tiger," "Alvin's Harmonica" by the Chipmunks, and "A Fool Such As I" by Elvis. A novelty tune based on Edd Byrnes's character on "77 Sunset Strip," "Kookie, Kookie (Lend Me Your Comb)," was recorded by Byrnes and Connie Stevens.

12

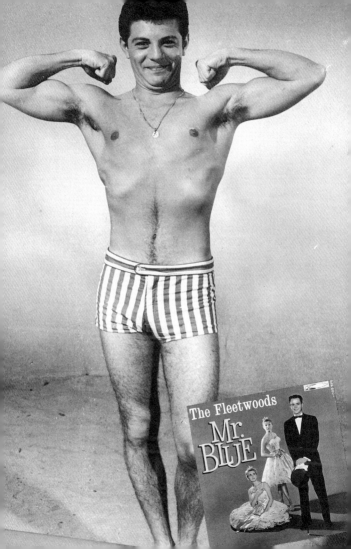

The Fleetwoods
Mr. BLUE

fiction

1. **exodus**
   by leon uris

2. **doctor zhivago**
   by boris pasternak

3. **hawaii**
   by james michener

4. **advise and consent**
   by allen drury

5. **lady chatterley's lover**
   by d. h. lawrence

6. **the ugly american**
   by william lederer and
   eugene burdick

7. **dear and glorious physician**
   by taylor caldwell

8. **lolita**
   by vladimir nabokov

9. **mrs. 'arris goes to paris**
   by paul gallico

10. **poor no more**
    by robert ruark

bestselling

books

nonfiction

1. **'twixt twelve and twenty**
   by pat boone

2. **folk medicine**
   by d. c. jarvis

3. **for 2 cents plain**
   by harry golden

4. **the status seekers**
   by vance packard

5. **act one**
   by moss hart

6. **charley weaver's letters
   from mamma arquette**
   (actor and "tonight" show guest)

7. **elements of style**
   by william strunk, jr.,
   and e. b. white

8. **the general foods
   kitchens cookbook**

9. **only in america**
   by harry golden

10. **mine enemy grows older**
    by alexander king

15

Major-league baseball had an action-packed season. The Los Angeles Dodgers gave the state of California its first world championship. The Dodgers had placed seventh in the NL in 1958, their first season after the franchise moved from Brooklyn, but they put the Milwaukee Braves away in the pennant race and then whipped the Chicago White Sox in the Series, four games to two. The White Sox had just won their first AL title in 40 years. Sox star was Ted Kluszewski. For Los Angeles, Johnny Podres, Gil Hodges, Don Drysdale, and Duke Snider led the magic names.

GOLF was a young man's game in 1959. Gary Player, 23, a pro from Johannesburg, South Africa, became the British Open champ, the youngest to take that title. In the U.S., Ohio State junior Jack Nicklaus, 19, became the youngest player in 50 years to win the U.S. amateur championship. William Casper, Jr., of California won the U.S. Open held at Winged Foot in June, despite a sudden chill and winds of 25 mph on the course. Mary Kathryn "Mickey" Wright retained women's USGA championship honors. Art Wall, Jr., of Pennsylvania was the leading pro golfer of the year, with winnings of approximately $50,000. He had a spectacular victory over Cary Middlecoff at the Masters in Augusta, Georgia.

In college football, attendance was up. Several rule changes were introduced: One was the increase of the space between goal posts by 4' 10", resulting in increased numbers of field goal attempts. The substitution rule was relaxed; anytime the clock was stopped, a player could be substituted without penalty. The number of time-outs allowed was increased from 4 to 5 per half. Bill Cannon, Louisiana State University halfback, won the Heisman trophy.

sports

BOXING

The sport had a rough year. Boxing was investigated by the Kefauver crime committee; there were grand jury hearings in New York, and federal indictments in California. Attendance was relatively low, and Los Angeles was replacing New York as boxing capital of the country. Ingemar Johansson of Sweden dethroned heavyweight champ Floyd Patterson in a bout at Yankee Stadium June 26, 1959. A scandal followed the fight; it involved racketeering and irregularities by the promoters.

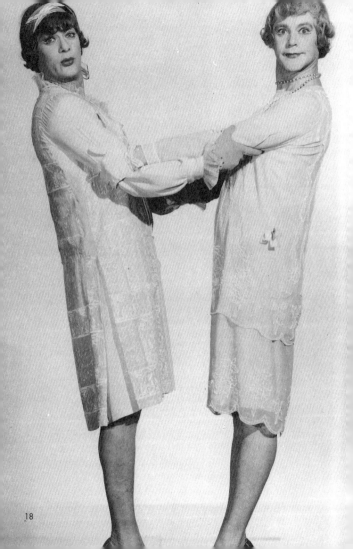

The spectacular **Ben-Hur** cleanly swept the Oscars. It garnered Best Picture honors, Best Direction for **William Wyler**, Best Actor **Charlton Heston**, Best Supporting Actor **Hugh Griffith**, color cinematography Oscar, film editing, art direction, costume (color), and scoring honors. The divine **Simone Signoret** was named Best Actress for *Room at the Top*. She won over Doris Day *(Pillow Talk)*, Audrey Hepburn *(The Nun's Story)*, and Katharine Hepburn and Elizabeth Taylor, both nominated for *Suddenly, Last Summer*. **Shelley Winters** won Supporting Actress honors for her role in *The Diary of Anne Frank*. Best song was **"High Hopes,"** by James Van Heusen and Sammy Cahn, from the movie *A Hole in the Head*.

Top Grossing Films of 1959 and their earnings
1. **Auntie Mame** $8,800,000
2. **Shaggy Dog** $7,800,000
3. **Some Like It Hot** $7,000,000
4. **Imitation of Life** $6,200,000
5. **The Nun's Story** $6,000,000
6. **Anatomy of a Murder** $5,250,000
7. **North by Northwest** $5,250,000
8. **Rio Bravo** $5,200,000
9. **Sleeping Beauty** $4,300,000
10. **Some Came Running** $4,200,000

movies

Top 10 box-office stars of 1959

1. Rock Hudson
2. Cary Grant
3. James Stewart
4. Doris Day
5. Debbie Reynolds

6. Glenn Ford
7. Frank Sinatra
8. John Wayne
9. Jerry Lewis
10. Susan Hayward

cars

After years of longer, lower, and finnier cars, the compact car started to emerge. There were more than 300 different models available, with prices ranging from $1,675 for a two-door Rambler to $12,000 for the Cadillac Special Brougham. The biggest gains were registered for Studebaker-Packard, whose Lark series made great sales gains. AMC's Ramblers sold well. Chevrolet introduced the revolutionary **Corvair** compact, with a rear-mounted air-cooled engine. Ford followed suit with the Falcon, and Chrysler produced the Valiant.

21

In menswear, the Continental look began to
challenge the Ivy League style; it featured a two-button, single-
breasted jacket style, a bit shorter with slashed pockets and semi-
peaked lapels. In sportswear, olive green and gold were big, and
there was great demand for lightweight sport coats, especially in
Indian Madras fabric. Wash-and-wear suits were popular, especially in the lower price ranges.

The controversial **sack and chemise** silhouettes did not disappear, but waistlines started to reemerge. Wide belts were a popular fashion feature, as were sashes and cummerbunds. Chanel's influence was omnipresent. The little hip-length suit jacket with contrasting binding and brass buttons was a true classic. Large, bulbous sleeves, reminiscent of those on a space suit, were popular. Luxe touches of fur trimmed many outfits. Metallic brocades, cut velvet, and satin were popular fabrics for evening wear. The eight-button glove was the perfect accessory. Muted colors, like taupe and olive green, and brown were the predominant colors. White was the favorite for evening fashion.

Bows and headbands accented fashionable heads everywhere.

fashion

'59

final factoid

Barbie, the legendary teen doll, debuted in 1959.

credits

'59